THE GEOGRAPHY DETECTIVE INVESTIGATES

Seaside Towns

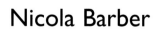

Nicola Barber

WAYLAND

Titles in *The Geography Detective Investigates* series
Rivers
Your Local Area
Mountains
Coastlines
Seaside Towns
Villages

First published in 2007 by Wayland

Copyright © Wayland 2007

Editor: Hayley Fairhead
Designer: Simon Morse
Cartoon artwork: Richard Hook

Wayland
338 Euston Road
London NW1 3BH

Wayland
Level 17/207 Kent Street
Sydney, NSW 2000

Barber, Nicola
    Seaside towns. - (The geography detective investigates)
    1. Seaside resorts - Juvenile literature
    I. Title
    307.7'6'09146

ISBN 978-0-7502-5051-1

Printed in China

Wayland is a division of Hachette Children's Books

Picture acknowledgements: AA World Travel Library p1, 9t © Laurie Campbell/NHPA p21 © Fridmar Damm/zefa/Corbis p24 Ecoscene p27 Courtesy of E.ON UK plc p26 © eye35/Alamy Images p16 GettyImages/ Hulton Archive p6, 7 © David Gowans/Alamy Images p14 © Angela Hampton/Collections p10 © Jeremy Horner/Corbis p22 Richard I'Anson/Lonely Planet Images p4 Kevin King/Ecoscene   p25 © Mike Kipling/Alamy Images p5 © Mike Kipling/Collections p12 Simon Lewis www.westcountryviews.co.uk p11 Kathy Lockley   p13 © Hans Peter Merten/Corbis Cover, p28 © Michael Milton/Collections p15 NRM – Pictorial Collection/Science & Society Picture Library p17t © Thierry Prat/Sygma/Corbis 9b Keith Pritchard/Collections p20, 29 Courtesy of Red Funnel Ferries p17b Rex Features p23© Paul Thompson; Eye Ubiquitous/ Corbis p8 © Sam Walsh/Collections   p19 © wsr/Alamy p18

With thanks to Jane Noad for reading the text

Cover: the harbour in Gardenstown, Scotland.

Contents

Words that appear in **bold** can be found in the glossary on page 30.

Answers to Sherlock Bones' questions can be found on page 31.

What are seaside towns?

From the earliest times, people have built settlements (places where people live) next to the sea. The sea was an important source of food. People travelled by boat to fish and to trade with other communities. Today, seaside settlements can be small fishing villages, towns or large cities.

Some seaside settlements have grown so large they have become major cities. For example, Sydney, on the east coast of Australia, started in 1788 as a small settlement of prisoners brought in from Britain. Today, it is the largest city in Australia with over 4 million inhabitants. Other seaside settlements have remained small, sometimes because their location meant that growth was difficult. For example, some seaside villages are built on steep cliffs rising up from the sea or in narrow river valleys that run down to the sea.

The city of Sydney has grown up around a natural harbour on the east coast of Australia.

With over 12,000 km of coastline, the UK has lots of different seaside towns. Some started as small fishing villages and still make their living from fishing. Others are busy ports and **harbours**. Today, many seaside towns in the UK are **resorts** which mostly make their living from tourism.

DETECTIVE WORK
Use an atlas or a map to find the nearest seaside town to where you live. Use the scale on the map to work out how far away it is. How would you get there from where you live? Is there a railway line or, if you were going to travel by car, is there a motorway?

Hartlepool is a busy port in northeast England.

FOCUS ON

Ports in the UK

Ports play an important part in the UK's **economy**. The busiest ports are on England's east coast – Grimsby and Immingham, Hartlepool, and London – while Milford Haven in Wales and Southampton on England's south coast are also major ports. Over 95 per cent of all **imports** and **exports** into and out of the UK pass through the country's ports.

How did seaside towns develop?

People originally settled along coastlines in **estuaries** and in natural **harbours**, or in places that were good for defence. For centuries, many coastal communities made their living from fishing, while other places became busy centres of trade. In the UK, during the nineteenth century, the seaside became fashionable for holidays, and the development of the railways allowed people to travel to popular seaside **resorts**.

Fishermen prepare their nets at Lowestoft, in 1950.

Early in their history, many seaside towns developed into busy ports, **importing** and **exporting** goods such as wool, wine, grain and wheat. In the sixteenth century, the need to defend the coastline and important ports led King Henry VIII to build a strong navy and a series of fortresses, many of which still survive today. Southsea Castle was built in 1544 to defend the town of Portsmouth, while Calshot and Hurst castles both defended the Solent (the stretch of water between the Isle of Wight and the mainland).

DETECTIVE WORK

See if you can find out about the history of a fishing community, and the life of a fisherman. To learn about fishing communities in the northeast of England, go to:

weblinks

www.waylinks.co.uk/series/ GeogDetective/Seaside

These wheeled huts were used for changing into swimming clothes at Southend-on-Sea, in 1900.

The fashion for seaside holidays in the UK had its beginnings in the late eighteenth century when people travelled to the seaside for their health. It was thought that drinking and bathing in seawater could cure a variety of illnesses. Scarborough in Yorkshire was one of the earliest seaside resorts.

While visits to the seaside were at first only for the wealthy, the arrival of trains and cheap travel in the nineteenth century (see pages 16–17) meant that many people could afford a holiday by the sea. During Victorian times, places such as Blackpool, Southend-on-Sea, Bournemouth and Skegness developed into major resorts with attractions such as theatres, music halls, seaside **promenades** and funfairs.

What are piers, promenades, causeways and breakwaters?

Seaside towns have many unique features and attractions. Some of these features, such as breakwaters, help to protect the town from the sea, while **piers** and **promenades** allow people to enjoy being by the seaside.

There are three piers in Blackpool. This one has a big wheel for spectacular rides.

Piers and promenades are built for people to enjoy the sea air, and have some fun! Piers are wooden or metal structures that are built out into the sea for people to walk along. The longest pier in the UK is at Southend-on-Sea, extending over 2 km into the sea. Promenades are wide paths that run alongside the seafront.

These pleasure boats are safely moored in Padstow, Cornwall.

Seaside towns often have **facilities** for boats. There may be **moorings** for just a few fishing or pleasure boats in a small **harbour**. Large towns may have a **marina** for people to keep their yachts and motor boats in safety. Even in places where there is a good natural harbour, people have often built features such as harbour walls or **breakwaters**. Breakwaters are man-made barriers that help to provide shelter from the sea during storms (see page 22).

A few seaside places have **causeways** – raised roads – that are covered over by the sea at high tides. One example is Mont St Michel off the coast of Normandy in France. In the past, the 1-km causeway that linked the island to the mainland was covered over at high tide, but at low tide it was possible to walk to the island. Today, the modern raised causeway is safe at all times, although the sands around the island can be very dangerous.

When the tide is low, cars can park safely along the causeway leading to Mont St Michel.

FOCUS ON

Guiding towers

Landmarks such as lighthouses and towers help to guide sailors, either warning them of hidden dangers such as rocks, or acting as markers for ships coming into **estuaries** or harbours. For example, the 26-metre tower at Walton-on-the-Naze in Essex dates back to 1721, and was built as a daytime mark to guide ships into Harwich harbour.

Who lives in seaside towns?

Seaside towns have a mixture of newcomers and residents whose families may have lived there for generations. People who live by the sea often enjoy a warm climate and a healthy **environment**, as well as local **facilities** such as golf clubs or outdoor swimming pools.

Older people often retire to seaside towns for the warm climate and facilities. As a result, some seaside towns have larger than average populations of people over 65. For example, in Bexhill-on-Sea in Sussex, 26 per cent of the population is retired – nearly double the national UK average of retired people. Eastbourne on the south coast also has a high percentage of retired people, around 25 per cent of the population.

The south coast of England is popular for retired people because of its warm climate.

Portscatho, on the Roseland Peninsula in Cornwall, is a popular place for holidays.

Many holidaymakers have favourite seaside towns that they like to visit year after year. Rather than stay in hotels, or rent houses, some people choose to buy second homes on the coast to use as holiday homes. In many places the increase in people buying holiday homes has pushed house prices up. This often makes it difficult for local people who cannot afford to buy houses in the town and may have to move away.

FOCUS ON

Seaside populations

Seaside towns in the UK can be large **resorts**, such as Bournemouth (with a population of 167,500) and Blackpool (142,300), or much smaller places, such as Berwick-upon-Tweed in the northeast of England (12,900) and Wells-next-the-Sea in Norfolk (2,451). Together with its near neighbour, Hove, Brighton is classed as a city, while ports such as Plymouth and Southampton are also cities.

What kind of buildings can you find in seaside towns?

Seaside towns have a wide range of buildings, from tiny cottages to grand hotels, modern museums to industrial buildings.

The buildings in the oldest parts of many seaside towns have changed little over the centuries. In the past, large numbers of seaside communities were based around fishing (see page 6), and fishermen's cottages lined the streets around every **harbour**. Today, places such as Staithes in Yorkshire still have old fishermen's houses. Many of these cottages are now holiday homes.

FOCUS ON

Special seaside buildings

Some seaside towns are home to dramatic modern buildings. In Bexhill-on-Sea, the De La Warr Pavilion was the first public building in the UK to be built in the **Modernist** style, out of steel and concrete. It was built in 1935, and has recently been **renovated** and reopened as an arts centre.

The De La Warr Pavilion in Bexhill-on-Sea attracts many visitors with its galleries, theatre, café and restaurant.

The UK's seaside **resorts** have some very grand buildings. Many were built during the nineteenth century, as seaside holidays first became fashionable (see page 7). In Brighton, **Regency**-style houses line the city's squares and terraces. Today, many of these buildings, which were once large houses or hotels, have been divided into apartments. Towards the end of the nineteenth century, the demand for seaside holidays was so great that huge hotels were built in many resorts. The Grand Hotel in Scarborough, Yorkshire, was the largest in Europe when it was completed in 1867, with 12 floors and 365 rooms. It is still a landmark in the town today.

The Grand Hotel in Scarborough was built to accommodate an increase in tourists.

DETECTIVE WORK
The most extraordinary building in Brighton is its Royal Pavilion. See if you can find out who it was built for and who designed it. What makes the building so exotic? What is it used for today? To find out more information about the Royal Pavilion, go to:

weblinks

www.waylinks.co.uk/series/
GeogDetective/Seaside

What jobs do people do in seaside towns?

The fishing industry continues to be very important in some seaside towns. Fraserburgh and Peterhead on the northeast coast of Scotland, and Fleetwood in northwest England are examples of towns that continue to have large fleets of fishing boats. The fishing industry employs lots of people in these places. Fishermen work on the boats, while on shore carpenters, electricians and engineers are vital to keep boats repaired and maintained.

DETECTIVE WORK

Where does the fish come from in your local supermarket? Check the labels at the fish counter in your local shop to find out where the fish were caught and landed, and how long it has taken for them to be transported. To find out more about the fish we eat, go to:

weblinks

www.waylinks.co.uk/series/GeogDetective/Seaside

Fishermen mend their nets on the harbourside in Peterhead, Scotland.

People who live in busy ports such as Southampton may work for port services, or for ferry companies. The Royal Navy also employs many people at its bases, for example in Portsmouth and Plymouth.

Tourism is very important for seaside towns. In the summer, shops, restaurants, hotels and beaches bustle with activity. As autumn draws in and the tourists leave, some businesses close down completely for the winter months. This means that in **resorts** that rely heavily on tourism for their income, many people are unemployed during winter, or are forced to go and look for jobs in neighbouring towns.

Resorts such as Blackpool and Bournemouth are trying to overcome this problem by becoming 'year-round' resorts, with **facilities** for conferences and other events. These resorts are building sports centres and other year-round attractions, as well as encouraging new businesses to help tackle unemployment.

A lifeguard keeps watch over the beach at Croyde, Devon.

What kinds of seasonal jobs are available in the summer in seaside resorts?

How do people travel to seaside towns?

The development of the railways during the nineteenth century allowed people to travel to the seaside. Travel by train was cheap, and trains could carry large numbers of people. Many railway lines were originally built to carry post, or to provide links to coastal industrial or mining areas. They also carried thousands of holidaymakers. A few small lines were built just for the holiday trade, for example the line to Padstow in Cornwall.

FOCUS ON

Trams and funiculars

In seaside towns, there are often unusual forms of transport to take visitors around the town, or up and down cliffs. Blackpool has 18 km of tramlines to carry passengers along its **promenade** and to nearby Fleetwood, while Llandudno in Wales has a **funicular railway** (called the Great Orme Tramway) to take people up and down the Great Orme hill.

This funicular railway is in Hastings on the south coast of England.

Why would a railway company use a picture of a seaside town on its poster?

This poster is for the North Eastern Railway, from 1910.

After World War II (1939–45), people began to use cars when they went on holiday to the coast, instead of travelling by train. Many of the smaller lines were closed down in the early 1960s, making it impossible to reach some seaside towns without travelling by road. Motorways such as the M5, which links Birmingham in the centre of the UK with Devon and Cornwall in the southwest, were constructed during the 1960s and 1970s.

The arrival of large numbers of cars has caused problems in some seaside towns. Many coastal places have narrow, winding streets which are not big enough for cars. In some places, car parks have been built on the outskirts of a town, with paths to take people on foot, or bus services to carry people into the centre.

This ferry transports people between the Isle of Wight and the UK mainland.

What attractions do seaside towns have?

All around the coast of the UK, there are seaside towns of historical and cultural interest. Many have great castles, for example at Bamburgh in Northumberland or St Mawes in Cornwall, and such landmarks are popular with visitors. Art galleries, museums and other attractions also help to bring visitors to a particular area. Arts festivals or other special events attract visitors to seaside towns, such as the annual arts festival in Tenby.

The village of Bamburgh has grown up around the castle, which was built over 1,000 years ago.

Seaside towns are often surrounded by beautiful scenery which is ideal for walking holidays. Sports such as sailing, windsurfing and surfing are popular all around the UK coast, particularly in places such as Newquay in Cornwall, which is known as the 'surf capital' of the UK. Most large **resorts** have good beaches. Many also offer attractions such as open-air swimming pools and **lidos**, donkey rides, amusement arcades and funfairs, sea-life centres and aquariums.

In the late twentieth century, many people started to go abroad for cheap holidays, instead of visiting the UK's seaside resorts. Some seaside resorts became very run-down, but today this situation is improving. Beaches have been cleaned up (see page 27) and local councils are spending money on improvements and **renovations** to attract visitors, and to improve the quality of life for residents. For example, Morecambe in Lancashire is home to the stunning Midland Hotel, which was the first **Art Deco** hotel in the UK when it was built in the 1930s. By the late 1990s the hotel had become very shabby and run-down, but now the hotel is being completely renovated.

DETECTIVE WORK

If you have visited a seaside town on holiday recently, can you list all the attractions on offer? How many of them did you visit during your holiday?

Blackpool Pleasure Beach has more than 125 rides, as well as restaurants and souvenir shops.

What wildlife can you spot at the seaside?

Look up into the sky at any seaside town and you will see seagulls flying around. Walk to the **harbour** wall and you may see people fishing. Look over the harbour wall and you may see a seal swimming in the waters below. Seaside towns are full of wildlife, and are good places from which to set off for more adventurous wildlife trips, such as whale-watching or bird-spotting.

Seagulls often find their food in household waste in seaside towns.

Around the coast of the UK, lots of seaside towns are located on or near **estuaries** which are home to a wide range of **wildfowl**, wading birds and **migratory** birds. The large sandy area of Morecambe Bay stretches for more than 300 sq km. Cockles, mussels, shrimps and worms live in the sand providing food for birds such as terns, pink-footed geese, shelducks and oystercatchers. Estuaries such as the Wash on the east coast of England, and the Severn on the west coast, are also important habitats for birds. Seagulls have adapted well to life in seaside towns by making their nests on rooftops.

Seals live all around the coast of Great Britain.

Boat trips take people to look at colonies of seabirds, and to spot **marine** animals such as seals, dolphins and whales. Whale-watching is popular off the western coast of Scotland, while grey seals and bottlenose dolphins can often be seen in Cardigan Bay, off the coast of Wales.

Why are seagulls attracted to seaside towns?

FOCUS ON

Brownsea Island

The seaside town of Poole sits on a spectacular natural harbour on the shores of the English Channel. There are several islands in the harbour, the largest of which is Brownsea Island. This island provides an important habitat for the red squirrel. This animal is in danger of disappearing from the mainland because of competition from the grey squirrel. There are no grey squirrels on Brownsea, and approximately 250 red squirrels live in the wooded areas of the island.

What are the hazards of living in seaside towns?

Seaside towns can be at risk during times of severe weather. In the UK, seaside towns have often suffered flooding when there have been bad storms. In other parts of the world, seaside communities live with the risk of **hurricanes**, and sometimes disasters, such as **tsunamis**.

A tsunami wave crashes onto a beach in Thailand, in December 2004.

In the UK, the worst storm flooding in recent history happened in 1953. In January of that year, strong winds coincided with a high tide to cause a **storm surge**. The sea water flooded large areas of eastern England and the Netherlands. More than 300 people died in England, while over 1,800 people died in the Netherlands.

FOCUS ON

The Asian tsunami

In December 2004, there was a massive earthquake beneath the sea near Sumatra in Indonesia. The earthquake caused several huge waves, called tsunamis, to spread across the Indian Ocean. These giant waves devastated coastal communities across southeast Asia, and killed more than 200,000 people.

The threat of flooding comes not only from the sea, but also from **flash floods**. In some places, settlements have grown up in narrow river valleys leading to the sea. One example is Boscastle in north Cornwall, which was hit by a flash flood in 2004. On 16 August, after five hours of torrential rain, the river that runs through the middle of Boscastle suddenly turned into a raging torrent. The water carried trees and cars into the sea and destroyed buildings in its path. The flood was so sudden that some people had to be rescued from the rooftops by helicoptor.

Why do flash floods happen so suddenly?

Around 75 cars and 6 buildings were washed into the sea during the flash flood at Boscastle.

Detective work

See if you can find out the name of the river in Boscastle. How will similar floods be prevented in the future? To find out more about the Boscastle floods, go to:

www.waylinks.co.uk/series/
GeogDetective/Seaside

How do people protect seaside towns from the sea?

E ver since people first began to settle next to the sea, they have built defences for protection from the power of the tide and waves. **Harbour** walls, sea walls, **groynes**, **breakwaters** and **reefs** are all designed to protect the coastline.

The Oosterschelde storm surge barrier in the Netherlands protects the land from the North Sea.

In some countries, for example the Netherlands, many towns lie on land that has been drained and reclaimed from the sea. In the Netherlands, reclaimed land is known as *polders*. The *polders* have always been protected by high sea walls, called **dykes**. After the terrible floods of 1953 (see page 22), the Dutch started to build a new set of sea defences called Deltaworks. Deltaworks is made up of many different types of sea defences, including huge **dams** and barriers to protect land from strong waves during storms.

(see page 22)

FOCUS ON

Global warming

Global warming is a danger for coastal communities all over the world, because of the effect on the level of the sea. As temperatures on Earth rise, more water from the icecaps at the North and South Poles is melting into the world's seas and oceans. As sea levels rise many coastal towns and cities could be flooded.

The movement of the waves along a coast means that coastlines are constantly being reshaped. The problem is that when coastal defences are built in one place, they usually have a 'knock-on' effect somewhere else. For example, in the 1990s, nine reefs were built off the coast at Sea Palling, Norfolk. The reefs are made from large boulders which reduce the impact of the waves. This protects the beach from **erosion**. Although the reefs have been a success for Sea Palling, further down the coast beaches are becoming more eroded.

This cliff has been eroded by the waves so that this house now stands close to the edge.

What will happen to this house?

DETECTIVE WORK

Happisburgh in Norfolk is in great danger of falling into the sea. It stands on sandy coastal cliffs which are slowly being eroded. See what you can find out about Happisburgh. For more information, go to:

weblinks

www.waylinks.co.uk/series/
GeogDetective/Seaside

How have people affected the seaside environment?

Ever since people first settled along the coast, they have changed the seaside **environment**. Sea defences can have an effect on the coastline many miles away. Sewage can pollute the sea and the shore. In the future, there are plans to use tidal power and wind power to provide increasing amounts of energy for the UK. All of these activities have an effect on the seaside environment.

FOCUS ON

Scroby Sands

Scroby Sands wind farm lies in the sea, about 3 km off Great Yarmouth in Norfolk. The 30 **wind turbines** have been built on a large sandbank in shallow water. In 2005, the wind farm produced enough energy to supply 36,000 homes. In the future, it is likely that much more of our energy will come from similar wind farms.

The wind turbines at Scroby Sands rise 108 m out of the water (to the tips of the blades).

Sea defences protect the coastline from the sea (see page 24). Sometimes these defences can have unexpected effects. An example is Minehead in Somerset. The old sea defences were destroyed by storms in 1995. They were replaced with a new sea wall and huge boulders to reduce the impact of large waves. However, the boulders affected the movement of the waves, and in 1999 Minehead's golden sandy beach was completely washed away. The beach was eventually replaced with over 300,000 tonnes of sand taken from the Bristol Channel.

Sandbanks beach near Poole is flying its Blue Flag to show that it is a clean place to swim.

Sewage is the waste-water that comes from our toilets, baths, sinks, washing machines and dishwashers. It flows into pipes called sewers, and is then treated to remove harmful **organisms** before being returned to the environment. However, in the past, large amounts of sewage were simply pumped into the sea, without being treated. In recent years, the quality of water in places where people swim has been improved.

Today, most seaside towns take great pride in the cleanliness of their beaches and the seawater. There are schemes, such as the Seaside Awards and the Blue Flag Programme, which reward beaches and **resorts** that are clean, well-maintained and safe.

Your project

If you've been doing the detective work throughout this book, you should have found lots of information about seaside towns, the people that live in them, their **environment** and their special features. You can bring all this work together by producing your own project about seaside towns.

The harbour at Gardenstown, in Scotland. Gardenstown was founded as a fishing village in 1720.

Topic questions

● Investigate the problems of providing sea defences for coastal settlements. What measures are being taken? How expensive is it to protect towns threatened by coastal **erosion**? How successful are the defences, and what are the possible knock-on effects?

● How are some seaside towns trying to overcome the problem of seasonal employment? What kinds of new businesses or new attractions help to provide year-round employment for local people?

● How are seaside towns taking measures to protect their local environment, both **marine** and coastal?

● Investigate the fishing industry in the UK. What are the main kinds of fish caught out of UK ports? Where are they sold? Which species are endangered?

You can find information at your local library and on the Internet. Look at the books and websites listed on page 31 for more ideas. When you have gathered the information you need, present it in an interesting way. You might like to use one of the ideas listed here.

Sherlock Bones has produced a project about Dunwich on the coast of Suffolk. He discovered that Dunwich was once a large port. Over the last 600 years much of the town has disappeared beneath the waves, as the cliffs which it was built upon have eroded.

Newquay in Cornwall has a beach with plenty of watersports to attract visitors.

Project presentation

● Design a brochure for a seaside town listing all of its attractions and **facilities**. You could include sections on the town's history, its transport links, and any other information that would be useful for a visitor.

● Write a report comparing two seaside towns. They could both be in the UK, or you could compare a UK town with one abroad. Examine how issues such as employment, preserving the town's heritage and protecting the environment are dealt with in the two places.

● Make a survey of your family and friends about seaside towns they have visited. Decide what questions you want to ask, then make a database to present your answers.

Glossary

Art Deco A style of art and architecture that developed in the 1920s and 1930s.

breakwater A wall built in the sea to reduce the impact of breaking waves.

causeway A raised road that may sometimes be covered by water.

dam A wall built to hold back the water of a river.

dyke A large wall built to keep out the sea.

economy A country's economy is the money it gets from its businesses and industries.

environment The world around us.

erosion The wearing away of rocks by the action of wind and water.

estuary A place where a river flows out into the sea.

export A product that is sold and transported to another country.

facility A service, a building or a piece of equipment that allows somone to do something.

flash flood A sudden flood caused by very heavy rainfall.

funicular railway A mountain railway with two cars joined by a cable that works by a system of weights, allowing the car travelling down the mountain to pull the other car up the mountain.

global warming The warming of the atmosphere around Earth as a result of the increased number of greenhouse gases, such as carbon dioxide, in the air.

groyne A barrier built at right angles to a beach to prevent sand from being eroded by the movement of the waves.

harbour A place on the coast where boats can be kept in safety.

hurricane A severe tropical storm.

import A product that is purchased and brought from another country.

lido An open-air swimming pool, often by or near the sea.

marina A place with floating walkways where pleasure boats are kept.

marine To do with the sea.

migratory Describes birds (or other animals) that migrate – move from one place to another depending on the season.

Modernist A style of architecture that developed in the twentieth century.

mooring A rope that is fixed to the seabed and attached to a float on the surface for a boat to tie up to.

organism A living thing.

pier A wooden or metal structure at a seaside resort that is built out into the sea for people to walk along, and for them to visit amusements, shops and restaurants.

promenade A wide path along the seafront in a seaside resort.

reef An underwater barrier.

Regency Describes the period from 1811 to 1820 when Britain was ruled by the Prince Regent, later King George IV, and the styles of art and architecture from that period.

renovate To repair and restore something.

resort A place, often by the sea, where people go for their holidays.

storm surge Flooding caused by a combination of a very high tide and severe gales.

tsunami A series of big ocean waves, often caused by an undersea earthquake or volcanic eruption, or by a landslide.

wildfowl Birds such as ducks and geese.

Answers

Page 15 During the summer tourist season, people can find work as lifeguards on the beaches, sports instructors, working for equipment hire shops, chambermaids in hotels, waiting on tables in cafés and restaurants, or selling ice creams.

Page 17 The railways used the attractions of seaside towns to persuade people to travel on their trains. Such posters were very popular in the late nineteenth and early twentieth centuries.

Page 21 Seagulls like to nest on rooftops and often find food in rubbish tips and waste bins. They can become a nuisance, and sometimes it is necessary to control their numbers.

Page 23 **Flash floods** usually happen as a result of extremely heavy rainfall. The ground cannot absorb all the water, and the result is sudden and often violent floods which can be very dangerous for people.

Page 25 The cliffs at Happisburgh are being **eroded** by the movement of the sea. As the cliff disappears beneath it, the house will eventually fall into the sea.

Further Information

Books to read:
Coast: A Celebration of Britain's Coastal Heritage
by Christopher Somerville
(BBC Books, 2005)

Exploring Seaside Towns
by Katie Orchard
(Wayland, 2004)

The Geography Detective Investigates: Coastlines
by Jen Green
(Wayland, 2007)

Websites:
Marine Network of Friends of the Earth:
www.marinet.org.uk/index.html

Information about the floods of 1953:
www.bbc.co.uk/weather/features/understanding/1953_flood.shtml

BBC magazine: *Seaside Life*:
news.bbc.co.uk/1/hi/magazine/5260198.stm

Department for Environment, Food and Rural Affairs:
www.defra.gov.uk/environment/water/quality/bathing/default.htm

Deltaworks online:
www.deltawerken.com/The-Deltaplan-/92.html

Fraserburgh town website
www.visitfraserburgh.com/index.htm

History of fishing in Polperro:
www.polperro.org/fishing.html

Internet geography:
www.geography.learnontheinternet.co.uk/topics/holdernesscoast.html

Peterhead port authority:
www.peterheadport.co.uk/

Seaside travel and nostalgia site:
www.seasidehistory.co.uk/index.html

Index

The Geography Detective Investigates

Contents of all books in the series:

WAYLAND